DINOSAUR ABC COLORING BOOK

BY LLYN HUNTER

DOVER PUBLICATIONS, INC., NEW YORK

ACKNOWLEDGMENT

The author wishes to thank Dr. Lawrence G. Barnes of the Vertebrate Paleontology Department of the Los Angeles County Museum of Natural History for supplying information used in the note on the "X-ray."

Bibliographical Note

Dinosaur ABC Coloring Book is a new work, first published by Dover Publications, Inc., in 1988.

International Standard Book Number
ISBN-13: 978-0-486-25786-0
ISBN-10: 0-486-25786-X

Manufactured in the United States by Courier Corporation
25786X17   2013
www.doverpublications.com

INTRODUCTION

No one has ever seen a dinosaur. We know them only from fossilized remains, yet dinosaurs are more familiar to most people than many living animals. It is not hard to discover why. Dinosaurs dominated the earth for 140 million years, in an age when the shape and position of the continents, as well as the climate and vegetation of the world, were very different from what they are now. The picture of an entirely different earth with entirely different life forms has captivated our collective imagination since the first fossilized dinosaur bones were identified as such in England in the early nineteenth century.

The 26 drawings in this book are arranged in alphabetical order, according to the first letter of the name of the principal dinosaur in each picture. The 28 dinosaurs depicted (including one pterosaur, a type of flying reptile related to the dinosaurs), like all dinosaurs, were reptiles. Lizards, crocodiles, snakes, and turtles, reptiles as well, lived also at some time in the age of dinosaurs. Yet they continue to exist, while the last dinosaur died about 65 million years ago—why, no one knows for sure, although many scientists now believe it probably had largely to do with a sudden worldwide change in climate. The age in which dinosaurs lived—from about 225 million to about 65 million years ago—is called the *Mesozoic Era*. The Mesozoic Era is divided into three periods: the Triassic Period (225 to 193 million years ago), when dinosaurs first appeared (about 205 million years ago); the Jurassic Period (193 to 136 million years ago),

when an enormous number of new species of dinosaurs evolved, including huge plant-eating beasts like Brachiosaurus; and the Cretaceous Period (136 to 65 million years ago), when the most fearsome predatory dinosaurs (like Tyrannosaurus) lived and at the end of which the last dinosaurs died out.

Besides indicating the particular period in which a given dinosaur lived, the notes on the dinosaurs in the drawings (these notes follow "A Note on Dinosaur Color") also give the pronunciation of the dinosaur's name, the meaning of the name in English (*dinosaur*, by the way, means "terrible lizard"), the size of the animal, and, finally, its "location," that is, where fossils have been discovered. This needs some explanation. To take one example, the location of Apatosaurus is given as "western United States." Naturally, there was no United States 150 million years ago. But it is more important to remember that the present-day arid, mountainous country where the Apatosaurus fossils were discovered bears no resemblance to the relatively flat, wet, warm, vegetation-covered landscape in the same location 150 million years ago, when this dinosaur lived. The duration of 150 million years—some 500 times as long as the time since our first true human ancestors (*Homo sapiens*) appeared on the earth—is long enough for major changes to have occurred in the surface and shape of the land, in worldwide climate, and in the nature of plant life covering the earth.

A NOTE ON DINOSAUR COLOR

What color is a dinosaur? That's a very good question. A major part of a paleontologist's job is to discover the answers to questions like this about animals that lived millions of years ago. Unfortunately, this question may be the most difficult one to answer.

When dinosaurs are discovered, their entire bodies are not found but rather their skeletons, the bone of which has been replaced by stone through chemical action over millions of years. Sometimes a cast of an animal's skin, a kind of fingerprint left in stone, is found. Otherwise, we can only guess at what the skin of a dinosaur looked like.

The way scientists make guesses about dinosaurs that are likely to be close to fact is by comparing them with present-day animals that have similar habits. For example, we know from the bone structure, teeth, and claws of Deinonychus that it was a hunting dinosaur. Many hunting animals today, like the cheetah, have spots to keep them concealed in foliage until they are ready to attack. This suggests that

Deinonychus may have had spots or similar camouflaging marks.

On the other hand, the rhinoceroslike Triceratops, armed with several sharp, massive horns, might not have needed any skin pattern at all, since it had nothing to hide from. While again, the small plant-eating Fabrosaurus would have needed camouflage to hide it from larger, carnivorous dinosaurs.

Though many artists like to depict dinosaurs with a lot of green in their skins, a number were probably colored in a variety of earth tones like brown, gray, yellow, orange, red, and black. But the fact is, we just don't know what color these ancient reptiles were. They could have been more colorful than a rainbow.

So here's your chance to be an amateur paleontologist. Read the information that follows about each of these dinosaurs. Then *you* decide what color each dinosaur should be!

NOTES ON THE DINOSAURS

A *Apatosaurus* (ah-PAT-uh-SAWR-us, "deceptive lizard"). Time: Late Jurassic. Length: 70 feet. Height: 15 feet at shoulder. Location: western United States. Apatosaurus was a huge sauropod ("lizard foot," a type of saurischian, or "lizard-hipped" dinosaur) that fed on soft, mostly aquatic plants. For about a century this beast was

thought to possess a head like that of Camarasaurus, another sauropod. This confusion resulted from the accidental lumping together of fossil remains of the two dinosaurs. Until the error was corrected, Apatosaurus was generally called *Brontosaurus*, a name most people will recognize.

B Brachiosaurus (BRAK-ee-uh-SAWR-us, "arm lizard"). Time: Late Jurassic. Length: 75 feet. Height: 40 feet to top of head. Location: western United States, Algeria, Tanzania.

The Brachiosaurus was one of the largest dinosaurs that ever lived. Its long forelegs, unlike those of most dinosaurs, were the reason for its name, "arm lizard." Because of its long neck and snorkel-like nostrils on the top of its head, Brachiosaurus was once thought to live submerged in water. Today paleontologists believe that it was more like a giant giraffe, browsing on leaves near the top of tall trees.

C Corythosaurus (ko-rith-o-SAWR-us, "helmet lizard"). Time: Late Cretaceous. Length: 33 feet. Location: western United States, western Canada.

The most interesting feature of Corythosaurus is its flat, hollow crest. There are many theories about the purpose of this "helmet." The most accepted one is that the crest was a visual signal identifying the lambeosaurine hadrosaurid (crested duck-billed dinosaur) to other dinosaurs, as well as separating males, females, and young within a given species. It is also thought that the hollow cavity within the crest acted as a resonator to amplify the bellowing sounds these animals probably made.

D Deinonychus (dy-NON-i-kus or dy-no-NIKE-us, "terrible claw"). Time: Early Cretaceous. Length: 8–13 feet. Location: western United States.

Though it was a relatively small dinosaur, Deinonychus was the perfect hunting machine. Its large head with sharp serrated teeth, its heavy, curved claws on its forelimbs, and its strong hind legs, each armed with a five-inch-long sickle-shaped claw, made the Deinonychus a fierce predator. It is believed that Deinonychus traveled in packs and hunted as wild dogs do today. Several would attack a young, weak, or poorly armed dinosaur many times their own size and share the meal among the group.

E Eoceratops (EE-o-SER-a-tops, "earliest horned face"). Time: Late Cretaceous. Location: western Canada.

Despite its name, Eoceratops was neither the first ceratopsid ("horned face") nor particularly early in the evolution of dinosaurs. In fact all ceratopsids, part of the larger group called ornithischians ("bird-hipped" dinosaurs), developed in the Late Cretaceous Period. The little that is known about Eoceratops comes from the half of a three-foot-long skull found in the Red Deer River region of Alberta, Canada. A large number of dinosaur skeletons have been found in this area, including those of many different species of Triceratops. Perhaps in the near future a full skeleton of Eoceratops will be found.

F Fabrosaurus (FAB-ruh-SAWR-us, "Fabre's lizard"). Time: Late Triassic or Early Jurassic. Length: 3 feet, 4 inches. Location: Lesotho, Africa.

The Fabrosaurus shown in this book is reconstructed by comparison with a close relative, the Lesothosaurus. In 1964, a fragment of a jawbone of Fabrosaurus with its teeth was found, and the name given to this dinosaur soon became part of that of a whole group of similar dinosaurs, the fabrosaurids. Fabrosaurus was a fast-moving plant-eating dinosaur that, like all ornithischians, had a special bone at the end of its lower jaw called a predentary bone. This was especially useful in cutting tough vegetation. Having no physical weapons or armor, the Fabrosaurus was most likely preyed upon by carnivorous dinosaurs. Its speed was its only defense.

G Gallimimus (gal-ih-MY-mus, "fowl mimic"). Time: Late Cretaceous. Length: 20 feet. Location: Mongolia.

The Gallimimus was one of the largest of a group of ostrichlike dinosaurs, the ornithomimosaurids. It is currently believed that these animals were omnivores, eating leaves, fruits, and seeds, as well as insects, reptiles, and other small animals. These reptiles had powerful rear legs designed for running, helping them escape their predators as well as catch small prey of their own. Their long, spindly arms and fingers were used to grasp branches, where they could get at fruits and buds.

H Hylaeosaurus (hy-LEE-uh-SAWR-us, "woodland lizard"). Time: Early Cretaceous. Length: 20 feet. Location: southern England.

Because it was discovered in the Tilgate forest of southern England, the Hylaeosaurus received the name of "woodland lizard." Very little is known about this dinosaur, for only the front half of its body was found. The tail region has been reconstructed by paleontologists on the basis of the corresponding parts of Polacanthoides, a similar dinosaur that lived at the same time. Hylaeosaurus was a tanklike reptile, well protected from its enemies by heavy armor. It was probably a docile creature that fed on low-lying plants and possibly insects.

I Iguanodon (i-GWAHN-uh-don, "iguana tooth"). Time: Early Cretaceous. Length: 25 feet–29 feet, 6 inches. Height: 15 feet–16 feet, 6 inches. Location: Europe, western United States, western Canada, north Africa, Mongolia.

The Iguanodon was a massive, plant-eating ornithischian with a birdlike beak and ridged cheek teeth similar to those of today's iguana lizard. The most interesting feature of this dinosaur is the large pointed thumb spike on each hand. These may have been used in mating or as defensive weapons. Because their skeletons have been found in large numbers, it is also thought that Iguanodon may have lived in large herds. This would have been added protection against predators.

J Jaxartosaurus (jax-AR-tuh-SAWR-us, "Jaxartes lizard"). Time: Late Cretaceous. Length: 30 feet. Location: USSR, China. (The Jaxartes was the ancient name of the Central Asian river now called the Syrdarya.)

The work in gaining an understanding of Jaxartosaurus is a good example of how paleontologists sometimes have to be "blind detectives." Only a few limb bones, vertebrae, and part of a skull have been found. From these few pieces and their location, scientists have been able to determine what kind of dinosaur Jaxartosaurus might have been, its size, and when it lived. Because a complete skull has not been discovered, details like the crest shown on the Jaxartosaurus in this book (it was a lambeosaurine hadrosaurid) can only be guessed at. As new bones are found, scientists may decide that this duckbill looked very different.

K Kentrosaurus (KEN-truh-SAWR-us, "spiked lizard"). Time: Late Jurassic. Length: 17 feet. Location: Tanzania.

Like its larger cousin the Stegosaurus, the Kentrosaurus had a double row of pointed flat plates running from the base of the skull to the middle of the back. From that point to the end of the tail, and on either side of the hips, it had sharp-pointed spikes, probably highly effective as defensive weapons. Like most ornithischians, Kentrosaurus was a plant eater.

L *Leptoceratops* (lep-toe-SER-uh-tops, "slim horned face"). Time: Late Cretaceous. Length: 6 feet. Height: 4 feet. Location: western Canada, western United States, Mongolia.

The Leptoceratops looked something like the Psittacosaurus ("parrot lizard") and the Protoceratops ("first horned face"). Like Psittacosaurus, it could walk on its hind legs and grasp with its hands, and it had the small frill (bony structure around the neck) and the somewhat longer forelimbs of Protoceratops. Though it looks as if Leptoceratops were an evolutionary step between these dinosaurs, scientists believe that they were really all just similar species.

M *Massospondylus* (mass-o-SPON-dih-lus, "massive vertebra"). Time: Late Triassic to Early Jurassic. Length: 13 feet. Location: southern Africa.

The long, slender bones (vertebrae) of its spinal column gave the Massospondylus its name. It normally walked on all four legs, but would rear up on two for browsing the tops of tree ferns. Each handlike paw also had a sharp, scythelike claw on each "thumb." This might have been used for pulling down branches or digging up roots, or possibly as a weapon. Massospondylus is also special in that it was among the first dinosaurs discovered to have had *gastroliths*—deliberately swallowed stomach stones that would grind up the plant material it ate. Some present-day birds swallow small stones for the same reason.

N *Nodosaurus* (NO-duh-SAWR-us, "node lizard"). Time: Mid-Cretaceous. Length: 18 feet. Location: western United States.

The "nodes" in the Nodosaurus' name were large bumps borne on armorlike skin plates. This ankylosaur (a type of ornithischian) was a heavily built dinosaur that browsed on low lying plants. Since it was probably a slow, ungainly animal, it relied on its armor-covered back for protection. Although, unlike its later relative the Ankylosaurus ("crooked lizard"), Nodosaurus lacked a club at the end of its tail, this massive appendage, covered with bumpy armor, still could have been a formidable weapon.

O *Ornithomimus* (or-nith-uh-MY-mus, "bird mimic"). Time: Late Cretaceous. Length: 11 feet, 6 inches–13 feet. Location: western Canada, western United States.

The forests and cypress swamps of Late Cretaceous western North America were the home of the slender, birdlike dinosaur Ornithomimus. It had very strong leg muscles and is thought to have been able to run faster than fifty miles an hour. Ornithomimus also had very large eyes and, for a dinosaur, a large brain, which, among other functions, probably gave it better coordination while running. Scientists now believe that some dinosaurs were far more intelligent than any present-day reptile.

P *Pachycephalosaurus* (pak-i-SEF-uh-lo-SAWR-us, "thick-headed lizard"). Time: Late Cretaceous. Length: 15–26 feet. Location: western United States.

The most unusual feature of this dinosaur was the dome of its skull, made of solid bone nine inches thick. Around 1955, it was suggested that the Pachycephalosaurus used its dense head as a battering ram. Later, paleontologists determined that this dinosaur may have behaved much as deer and goats do today, using their thick heads not only as a defense against predators but for head butting among themselves to establish dominance in a herd.

Q *Quetzalcoatlus* (ket-SOL-kuh-WAT-lus, "Aztec feathered-serpent god"). Time: Late Cretaceous. Wingspan: 33–50 feet. Location: western United States.

In 1972, in Big Bend National Park, Texas, some very special remains were found: those of a giant pterosaur, afterwards named Quetzalcoatlus. Before then, the Pteranodon ("winged toothless") with a wingspan of 39 feet, was thought to be the largest of the flying reptiles. In recent years it has been determined that many pterosaurs could probably walk in some fashion on land and flap their wings and glide when in the air, like modern birds. It now appears that Quetzalcoatlus, like vultures, spent much of its time soaring on rising currents of warm air and was a scavenger, feeding on the remains of dead dinosaurs and other creatures.

R *Riojasaurus* (ree-O-ha-SAWR-us, "Rioja lizard"). Time: Late Triassic. Length: 19–36 feet. Location: Argentina.

First discovered in La Rioja Province, Argentina, the Riojasaurus belongs to an early group of dinosaurs known as prosauropods. Unlike its close cousins the Massospondylus and the Plateosaurus ("flat lizard"), which could rear up on their hind legs, the Riojasaurus was restricted to walking and standing on all fours. Because it could not stretch to browse on higher foliage, this dinosaur must have eaten a diet of medium-height ferns and low-lying plants.

S *Stegosaurus* (steg-uh-SAWR-us, "roofed lizard"). Time: Late Jurassic. Length: 20–30 feet. Location: western United States.

The plant-eating Stegosaurus, an ornithischian, is one of the most familiar dinosaurs. For protection from the large flesh-eating dinosaurs, Stegosaurus had four sharp spikes projecting from its tail. The purpose of the large shingle-like plates that ran from the base of its skull and down its tail has been debated for years. It is currently thought that they served primarily as heat exchangers, regulating the reptile's body temperature. Stegosaurus is also known for its unusually small brain. Though it was only the size of a walnut, weighing 2.5–2.8 ounces, it must have been large enough for the dinosaur's needs, for Stegosaurus existed on earth for about ten million years!

T *Triceratops* (try-SER-uh-tops, "three-horned face"). Time: Late Cretaceous. Length: 25–30 feet. Location: western Canada, western United States.

Its sharp beak and scissorlike teeth made Triceratops capable of eating shrubs, palms, and other tough, fibrous vegetation of the Cretaceous Period. This rhinoceroslike reptile, among the largest of the ornithischians, is thought

(Text continued on page 32.) 5

Apatosaurus

6

Brachiosaurus

B

7

Corythosaurus

Deinonychus

9

E

Eoceratops

Fabrosaurus

F

11

Gallimimus

12

Hylaeosaurus

H

13

Iguanodon

Jaxartosaurus

15

Kentrosaurus

Leptoceratops

Massospondylus

18

Nodosaurus

19

Ornithomimus

Pachycephalosaurus

P

21

Quetzalcoatlus

Riojasaurus

R

23

Stegosaurus

Tyrannosaurus

Triceratops

25

Ultrasaurus

26

Velociraptor

Saurornithoides

V

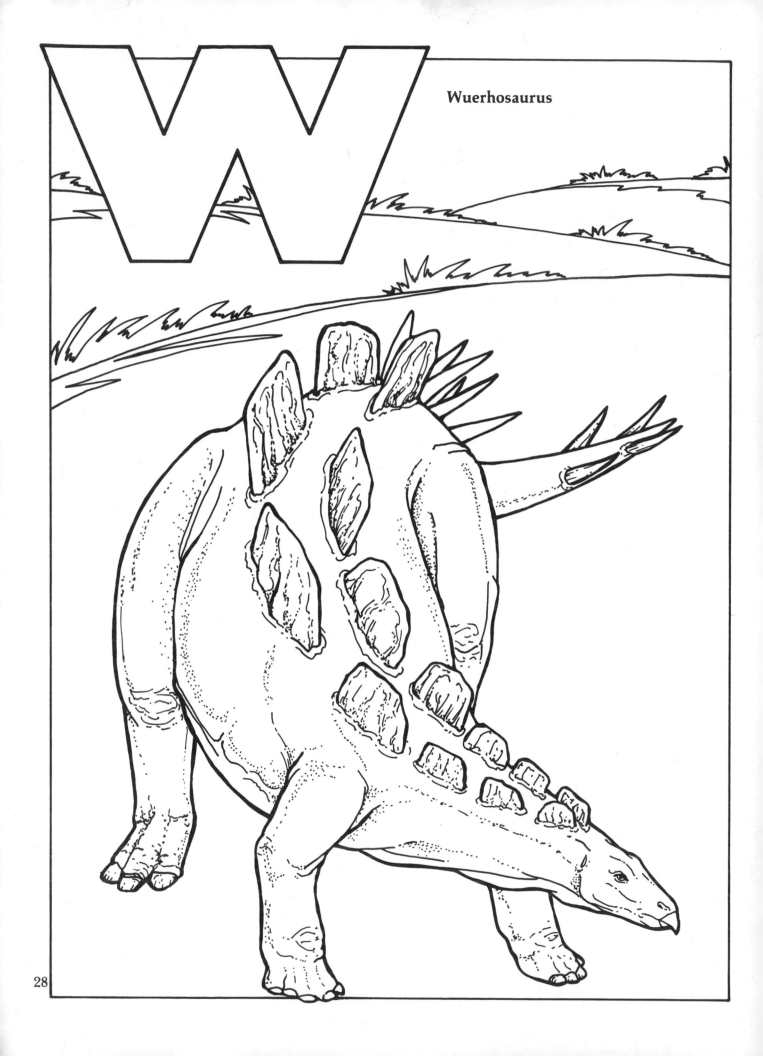

Wuerhosaurus

28

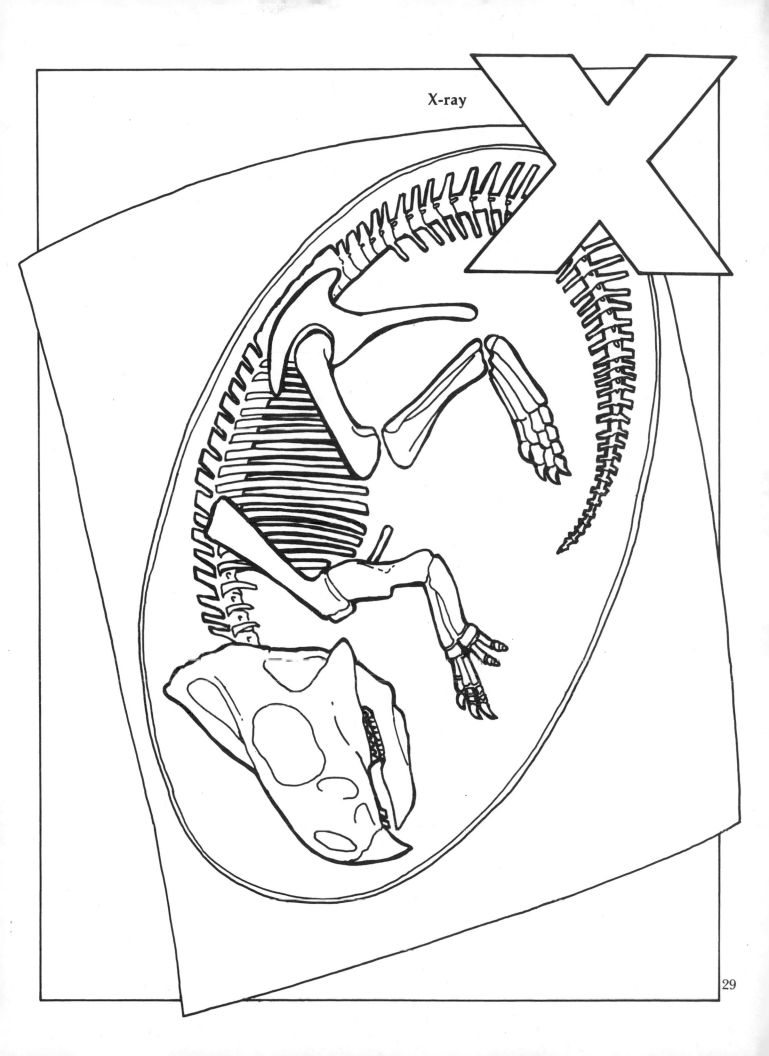

X-ray

Yunnanosaurus

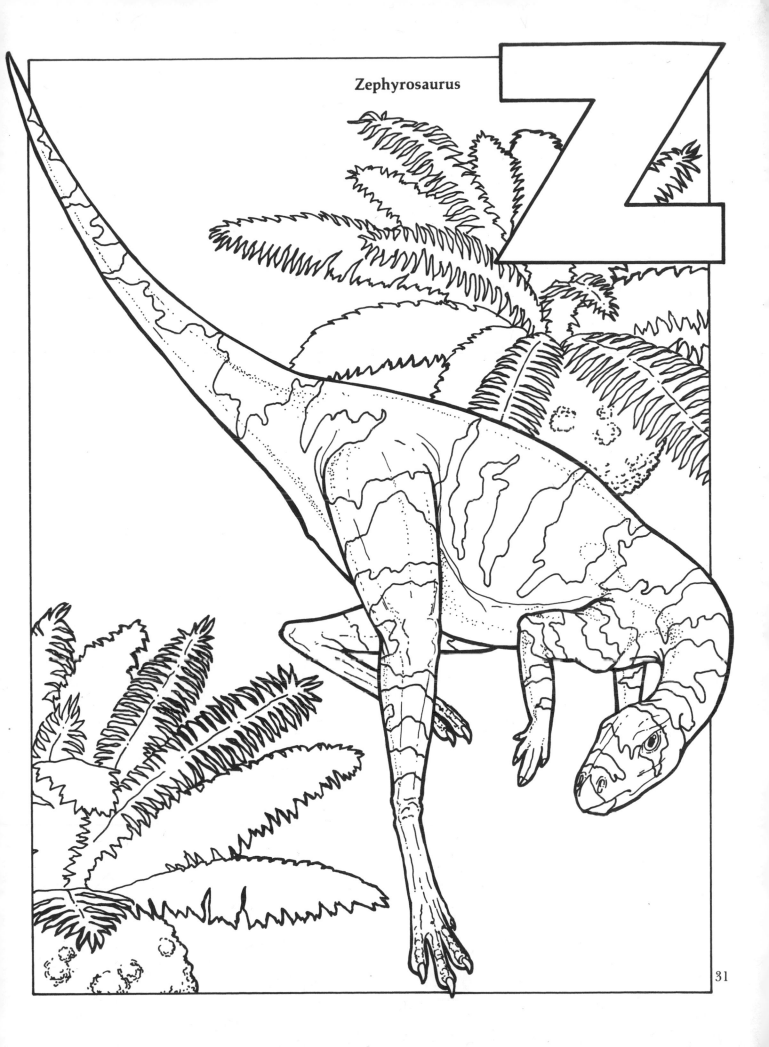

Zephyrosaurus

31

to have traveled in small herds, with adults protecting the young in times of danger. Though seemingly slow and heavy, the Triceratops could muster a forceful charge when confronted. With that kind of power behind such a formidable set of horns, Triceratops must have had very few predators.

Tyrannosaurus (tye-RAN-uh-SAWR-us, "tyrant lizard"). Time: Late Cretaceous. Length: 39–50 feet. Height: 18 feet, 6 inches. Location: western Canada, western United States, China.

The *Tyrannosaurus* (often known by its full scientific name, *Tyrannosaurus rex*) is the largest carnivorous (meat-eating) animal ever to have roamed the earth. Its gigantic four-foot-long head with huge jaws bearing teeth up to six inches long must have made it a terrifying predator. Because of its massive body, ill-equipped for running, some paleontologists believe that this therapod (type of carnivorous saurischian) must have been a scavenger, feeding on dead animals. Most scientists, however, feel that this giant was capable of great bursts of speed, swiftly lunging at its prey as lions do today.

U *Ultrasaurus* (UL-truh-SAWR-us, nonscientific name meaning "ultra lizard"). Time: Late Jurassic. Length: about 100 feet. Height: 50–60 feet. Location: western United States.

Though it has not been officially "described" or given a scientific name, the Ultrasaurus, discovered in 1979, is, at least for the present, the largest dinosaur known to have existed. So far, only the shoulder blade, measuring nine feet, vertebrae measuring five feet, and various other bones have been found. Because of the similarity in bone shape, Ultrasaurus is thought to be a close relative of Brachiosaurus, but it would have been about one-third larger than its already gigantic cousin. To give an idea of its size, the Ultrasaurus in this book is shown standing next to a Stegosaurus.

V *Velociraptor* (veh-LOSS-i-RAP-tor, "swift plunderer"). Time: Late Cretaceous. Length: 6 feet. Location: USSR, China, Mongolia.

The Velociraptor was a meat-eating dinosaur about the size of a man, closely related to Deinonychus. In 1971 a complete skeleton of the Velociraptor was found, with the skull of a Protoceratops clutched in its forelimbs. This pair of skeletons gives paleontologists the clue that Velociraptor possibly fed on Protoceratops and its eggs. One of the Velociraptors pictured in this book is shown attacking a Saurornithoides (sawr-or-ni-THOID-eez, "birdlike lizard"), another carnivorous dinosaur that probably competed with the Velociraptor for food.

W *Wuerhosaurus* (WER-ho-sawr-us, "Wuerho lizard"). Time: Early Cretaceous. Length: 20 feet. Location: western China.

Discovered in 1973 in the Wuerho District of Sinkiang, China, the Wuerhosaurus was one of the first stegosaurid (plated) dinosaurs found to prove that its kind did not become totally extinct during the Late Jurassic Period. Though only a few fragments of the skeleton were discovered, the Wuerhosaurus seems to have had long, low plates and a wider hip girdle than earlier species. Long, thin spikes rose on its back above its hips to offer additional protection from predators.

X *X-ray*

The X-ray is of course not the name of a dinosaur but that of an extremely important tool for the paleontologist. With it he can determine the size and shape of a dinosaur's brain case or see the cross section of a leg bone without having to cut apart valuable fossils. The X-ray photograph depicted in this book is that of a fossilized Protoceratops egg. The X-ray shows the unborn baby dinosaur's skeleton without necessitating the destruction of the stone egg around it.

Y *Yunnanosaurus* (YOU-non-uh-SAWR-us, "Yunnan lizard"). Time: Early Jurassic. Length: 20 feet. Location: Yunnan Province in southern China.

It was once thought that Yunnanosaurus was a plateosaurid, and it was identified with the prosauropod Lufengosaurus (named for another Chinese location). Recently, though, special studies of the Yunnanosaurus' teeth have shown that they were chisel-like, similar to those of the Brachiosaurus. This does not mean that the Yunnanosaurus is closely related to the giant sauropod but rather that it evolved along similar lines, eventually developing a similar diet and eating habits. This discovery also placed Yunnanosaurus in a group of its own.

Z *Zephyrosaurus* (ZEF-er-o-SAWR-us, "west-wind lizard"). Time: Early Cretaceous. Length: 6 feet. Location: western United States.

The Zephyrosaurus was a small ornithischian very similar in form to its better-known relative, the Hypsilophodon ("high ridge tooth"). The special characteristic of this plant-eating dinosaur was its teeth. The cheek teeth of Zephyrosaurus were self-sharpening. They would maintain their cutting edges by grinding against each other; new teeth were constantly growing in to replace those that had been ground down. Some scientists feel that these special teeth enabled Zephyrosaurus to take the ecological place of the fabrosaurids, early Jurassic dinosaurs that had died out millions of years before Zephyrosaurus came to exist.

SOURCES

The following is a list of books used as sources for most of the information in the above notes. Readers wishing to learn more will find in these books many additional fascinating facts about dinosaurs.

Benton, Dr. Michael. *The Dinosaur Encyclopedia*. New York: Wanderer Books, 1984.

The Diagram Group [David Lambert]. *A Field Guide to Dinosaurs*. New York: Avon Books, 1983.

Glut, Donald F. *The New Dinosaur Dictionary*. New Jersey: Citadel Press, 1982.

Norman, Dr. David. *The Illustrated Encyclopedia of Dinosaurs*. New York: Crescent Books, 1985.

Sattler, Helen Roney. *The Illustrated Dinosaur Dictionary*. New York: Lothrop, Lee & Shepard, 1983.